gentle
fictions

sherwin
tjia

P9-DEM-614

INSOMNIAC PRESS

Edited by Lynn Crosbie
Copy-edited by Catherine Jenkins
Designed by Sherwin Tjia

**National Library of Canada Cataloguing in Publication
Data**

  Tjia, Sherwin, 1975–
      Gentle Fictions

  Poems.
  ISBN 1-894663-13-6

  I. Title.

  PS8589.J52G4 2001   C811'.6   C2001-902146-1
  PR9199.4.T56G4 2001

The publisher and the author gratefully acknowledges
the support of the Canada Council, the Ontario Arts
Council and Department of Canadian Heritage through the
Book Publishing Industry Development Program.

Printed and bound in Canada

Insomniac Press, 192 Spadina Avenue, Suite 403,
Toronto, Ontario, Canada, M5T 2C2
www.insomniacpress.com

contents

voodoo

It is Wednesday, March 10, 1999
and Gail Cheshire, brown-haired with
blue eyes, a pretty girl by anyone's standards,
lives at 76 Buckingham Ave. in Toronto, Ontario.
The postal code is M4N 1R4.
Her phone number is (416) 920-9741.
You can call her or write her a letter.
She may be amused and invite you over,
or be frightened enough by your solicitation
to call the police.

She has a sister named Maeve.
They both attend Branksome Hall,
an upper-class private school just off
Mount Pleasant Rd. in the heart of
Toronto's wealthiest neighbourhood.
A beautiful school by anyone's standards.

At 10 Elm Ave., Branksome Hall spans both
sides of the road, surrounded by green
trees and bountiful bushes. You can attend
Branksome as well if you are a young girl
living in Toronto, whose parents are
willing to spend $14,950 CDN
per year on your education.

By the time you read this,
Gail Cheshire may not be living
at this address. Maybe the phone
number will have been changed. Maybe
she will have gone off to the university
or college of her choice. Maybe she'll
have a boyfriend, or a girlfriend.

Maybe some calamity will have entered the lives
of the Cheshire household. Maybe her dad who's a doctor
will be found too late with a tumour in his brain.
Maybe bad things happen to good people.

Maybe dirty boys and dirty girls are calling her
up and telling her astonishing things. Maybe she
is receiving a lot of mail. Maybe she will become
a cult celebrity without knowing why. Maybe she will
blame herself. Maybe she will be kidnapped by a
crazed and obsessed fan. Maybe she will be found
on his shrine to her. Maybe someone has taken her
picture and stolen her soul. Maybe she really feels
way too open right now.

TREASURE HUNT

Hello. I am a 48 yr. old MWM, 5'11", 160lbs, dirty blond hair, blue eyes, have a nice build, am fun to be with and financially secure from the Burlington area. I am a passionate music—lover and I have diverse musical tastes. I cook, am down to earth, spontaneous, intelligent and outgoing. I am looking to spend some time with my daughter, Sarah, shopping, basketball and so on. She is a SWF aged 15, 5'6", about 120lbs, very pretty, brown hair, blue eyes, slight build and a recreational smoker. Enjoys painting, rowing and museums. Avid collector of butterflies. She has been missing since Nov. 15, 1999, disappearing after school. Last seen wearing a St. Mary's school green uniform kilt (MacInnes Clan tartan) $45, St. Mary's blouse $25, school sweater $80, Club Monaco brown suede jacket $180, dark blue tights by Hanes $6, and Aldo loafers $120. She is possibly in the company of Jay Thomas Porter. D.O.B: Oct.13, 1974, eye colour: brown, hair colour: dark brown with bright red streaks. A sharp gentleman who knows his way around the city and needs a classy-looking woman to share unforgettable times. Distinguishing features: a gothic Celtic band resembling barbed wire around his right bicep. **Call 1-800-387-7962** toll-free if you have any information about this missing child. For the Club Monaco retail outlet nearest you, call **1-800-528-7228**. Call **212-752-7822 EXT 8194** ($1.95 per min.) to respond to this ad and leave a personal message. All calls are confidential.

CHILDREN & TEENS

FOR SALE

Girl, 10, white, 5'4", 118 lbs., speaks eng., $1500, 872-8842.

FOR SALE

Boy, 4, East Indian, ex. cond., like new, $500, 342-7475, eve.

FOR SALE

Girl, 8, small, responds to Angela, good cond., used once, $700. Mike @ 889-1411.

FOR SALE

Girl, 7, tlt.-trained, comes with jumper, toys. Must see. $800, 272-5148.

FOR SALE

Boy, 15, 5'7", slim, big dick, Boston bred, used one season, comes w/ cage, $1700, 342-1009.

FOR SALE

Girl, 12, beautiful, never used, ex. cond., deb., small, many features, asking $1400, 272-4008.

LOST

Boy, 13, brown, 5'4", stocky, escaped 06/12/98 from Cornwall. May be wearing blue tracksuit. If found, please contact Ray @ 542-8466. $$$ Reward.

FOR SALE

Boy, 13, cute, starter, sleeps 2, wide-access, 6" draw, new clothes, clean, no diseases, ex. cond., perfect for couple, for more info: 872-2346. $1400 or best offer.

FOR SALE

Girl, as is, L, 7, $500, 482-8001 eve.

FOR SALE

Girl, 16, M, will trade, exp., needs work, make-up. Best offer, 925-1311.

FOR SALE

Assorted boys/girls, new to country, come w/ papers, will trade, med- and long-haired, need good homes. More info: 545-8662.

FOR SALE

Boy, 8, Asian, trained, toned, talkative. From good family. Financing available, $1000. 842-6443.

Before You Know It

for isabelle

i

"I love the wounded," she tells me. "Not because they're wounded," she says, "But because I am." Her availability is making me unreasonably happy. My guts are jumpy, like life is a many-coursed meal that I don't have the stomach for. Like this has happened before, like there is something I should do differently this time. By now it is three days later, and I am beginning to doubt that god will let me have this love.

I am holding onto my jar of gold stars, rubbing her ankles and making wishes. I want to bare my bellyful of wounds, hoping she'll kiss them and call them beautiful. She tells me she feels like she's dressing in drag when she dresses like a girl. I tell her I am a cat trapped in a dog's body, the kitten in me purring when she walks into the room.

"Do you like girls?" she asks me. "Yes," I breathe. She says, "Me too." Then she shows me her drawings that burn like trauma. I remember waiting by the changeroom door when she came out in shiny black, me thrown by the bloom and bliss of it, all so at once. "I'm going to leave my body to necrophiliacs," she tells me. "It's on my organ donor card."

We are sitting at a café by the métro. The soles of her shoes are layered cakes. People open-armed embrace. The girls in glasses and high-heeled boots are walking with limps. There is a bubbly boy with a balloon in the park across the street. Finally, she says, "I don't know about you, but I've got ugly needs." Night falls fast. The sun plummets faster than the eye can catch. Before you know it this grass will be glimmering with dew.

I can fit your whole fist in my mouth. Blind appetite disrupts our delicate ecosystems. This is my life as a lion. I want. That's never changed. I want someone who wants. We play games. You and your firstborn dance fearlessly on the ledges of roofs. I want to risk breaking both legs on this bet today. You take me to the edge to show me the view. I look down and thirteen stories seems not so far away.

Weeks later we were still feeding, still coming back for more. We were broken but mending on disturbed soil. We were mismatched knee socks lost in the laundry. We were hugging each other and not thinking of stopping.

ii

We are sitting in your living room listening to your housemate and her boyfriend have sex. You have your hand in mine. We are suddenly wide-eyed children. "They're at it," you whisper to me, when she begins to breathe fast. "Je t'aime, je t'aime," he moans. I can see him weeping. I can see him on his knees.

When I use the word love I feel more alive and closer to death. Love is like someone I just met who tells me he is a long-lost relative. He tells me he knew me when I was little. He tells me I was beautiful, beautiful. He used to play with me. How come I can't remember him? I would have remembered him. I know I would have.

We are on your couch. You rest your ankles on my knees and I am holding your feet. Later I rest my head on your lap. We are each other's end tables. "Tell me something about yourself that'll make me wet," you say. I tell you that Jesus appeared to me for a second last night. He said he was a porcelain teacup. People poured their pain into him, and when he was full, he wept.

You drink me like juice, like I am squeezed from a bottle. You guide me through the darkness of your living room, around tables, chairs, and into your tiny room. Rubbing baby oil on your back I say, "We are going to reek." You stretch your arms above your head. "We'll smell like babies," you smile.

Your room is small, but sex can still take us outside it. Making love gives us wings. "Flap!" you are shouting at me. "Flap!" Your legs are wings on my back. "Faster!" We are getting carried away. We are riding this bed out the window, we will crater this bed in the ground.

I am drinking you when you sing these songs. You stick your tongue inside my ear, and I plummet like a comet straight from the sky to your backyard. You are on your belly, breasts huddled like eggs underneath you. And I am full of a tenderness reserved for the softest girls.

Lace thick as cake is topping your stockings. I spend time living in your walk-in closet, these velvet dresses hanging like curtains on every side. Underneath all these covers I am smelling of you. My body is baked bread in the oven of your love, and I am all cheese and crackers.

iii

In the beginning you said to me, "We have a kiss to get over with."

Lights gently twinkle outside your window. *Slowdive* is playing on the stereo. We are sitting on your well-made bed, in your surprisingly sparse room, eating cereal. I concentrate very hard on my Fruit Loops, but you are staring at me. "Stay away from my housemate," you tell me. "She's a sociopath." You lift your stockinged foot out of your shoe to give it some air, then slide it back in.

Your warm tongue slips into me like spring thaw. Even my frozen cedars sweat. Intimate as your exposed underarm, the blasted grass shows itself for the first time in months. We dance softly, trying not to step on each other's toes. This dance, the one to teach us how to dance. This dance not about dancing, but about maintaining contact. Your feet mutter something below us.

Your body makes my body make sense. We cook each other like dishes we are going to eat. We stroke each other like aloe plants. Normally I float like a dreamy balloon just above my head, but undressing you pops it soundly. I am in awe of your upholstery. My night was a rope that tied itself at one end, untied itself at the other.

You throw your panties at me from across the room. "Smell them," you tell me. In mid-air I paw your soft thong down. You point your finger at them and smile all eager and awake. "They don't smell *bad*, do they?" I am fingering the damp spot. "Go ahead. Smell them," you insist. I bring the softly stained cotton gusset up to my nose. "Give them a good sniff," you coax. "Do it." I inhale it like it's steak with mushrooms. Hmm. Cumin and lime.

Your rubber-gloved finger is sinking even deeper into my golden puckered apple 'n spice asshole. We are breaking up every morning and making up every night. I don't know how we stand the tension, I don't know how we're going to stop.

"You're weird, you know?" you say to me. I put my hand on top of your head. "Weirder than you?" You smile at me, "I'm not weird." I nibble a little bit of flesh off the hard part of your pinky finger and swallow it. "Hey," you say. "That's cannibalism." I respond, "You say that now, but I've been watching you eat yourself for the past half hour."

The next morning, your dried secretions are caked in my pubic hair like white fat on an iron grill.

Navarino's is busy, but we find a table between two leafy plants. Fairfield Porter paintings are up, pictures so soft they coo. The cold has impregnated our clothes. We rumpled children struggle out of our furs. You look like you should be in a bar, with men in suits, sipping martinis with one leg crossed over the other, in that black mohair skirt.

Over generous sandwiches, I tell you I want to be rich and famous. You say to me, "Maybe the question isn't why you want to be so big, but rather, why it is you feel so small." We talk about stupid things. I love not giving these things a second thought as we mention them for the first. I love as the warm red soup slides down my throat like a boy on a slide, screaming all the way in fear and delight.

The sun comes in the window to sit on your shoulder like an animal, bouncing off my folded glasses nested in my toque, off our cups and spoons. We have our mutual jokes, code words. We've formed conspiracies. We have robbed large and important banks in our time with only our fingers and our tongues.

Co-Operative Housing

Today I met the man
in the basement, and
his cactus collection.
Maybe in 20 years he'll
save the world, but he's
a complete asshole today.
I can only wish that he
has a happy ending too.
He's saying, look at me—
I need someone to take care
of me, because I'm a sick fuck.
I need people to pet me and
play with me and tell me
I'm wonderful. Look what
happens when someone
spends too much
time alone.

There's a boy in the
attic who spends all
his time painting god.
Gold tips his brushes,
serenity on his lips.
He's always waiting for
the angels to come and
cover him with clouds.
He says, let me break you
so I can heal you so I
can break you again. Let
me kill you so I can drag
you back from death so you
can suffer again. Gold
paintings against emerald
green. His eyes match
the wallpaper, looking
out to the sea.

Walk-In Closet

on the floor
amongst her dirty underwear
we are spinning the bottle
with both our names in a hat
plush carpet like green grass
and while i am heavily focused
on freeing her well-behaved buttons
she is asking me if i have
a date for the spring dance
while outside the city murmurs itself
awake long before her parents stir
in the other room
and unfastening her bra is like
defusing a bomb
like finding the roadway in the forest
and she is chewing gum with
one breast hanging solo out of
her dress and i am on a full
tank out of new york with the
next rest area in fifty miles
and i tell her no, not yet, and
we take turns so tightly only
our luggage weighs us down
hoping that during this dawn
surrounded by trees
no state police car
takes pursuit
and no flashing light
finds us

Hanging There Like That

The prep school that I went to
had an Alexander Calder hanging, like
a spider, from the cafeteria ceiling.

He'd gone there years before,
donating the piece once he'd become
a big art world hotshot.

We covered his work in art class.
I'd scour library books, finding
pages of elegantly suspended mobiles.

The Calder revolved high above us,
silent as swimming fish, responding
to the tiniest eddies of air.

Last year they had the spring dance
in the cafeteria, and the committee
took an entire week to decorate.

Streamers, balloons, the works.
It looked great. They even painted
the Calder to match.

HEARTTHROBBER

She is breathing her life away in here. At 21, she is so cool she could-n't even give a shit about not caring. Touselling with the monsters in her head, she is Joan of Arc with a fashion sense. She wants out from behind the counter, to ask inappropriate questions of her customers. When asked if she would have done it, she said she would have liked to have had the time. Someone asks her for another café au lait with cinnamon. All the soft people standing around this enchantingly vulgar girl, who takes their money with one hand and makes change with the other. She wants to dash out the front door and join the sleepy blondes in their shiny black cars surfing through the runnels of snow like trout along Crescent street. The people pulsing, new love on everyone's lips. Her first kiss made her want to throw up. People remember her as the maddest girl in school. Her eighth grade prizewinning speech: I'd like to live in nuclear winter. She remembers every Enid Blyton adventure she's ever read. Every chapter. She's got talents. People tell her. She can be completely charming. You're going to do what she wants you to—and you're not going to mind. She is blessed with the insane cheekbones of the moment. She has a draw-erful of tissue-thin lacy underthings, a closetful of slinky little slip dresses, and she loves the way she smells. This from a girl, who had at one point, given up being a girl. Today her to-do list reads: hang out, dress up, make stuff, have do's, and have rivers of money flowing in the door. On her break she meticulously pens napkins full of her still-seedling dreams. The empire up and running. Correspondents in every country, registering the global local scene. Music festivals, magazines, records and media. Something for everyone. Pedestrian.com. She sits in the sun and says to herself, "Pretend you're tea. I am Bengal Spice, I love to seep into my surroundings, steep the world." She reads things and realizes that she is not outside of it. In the name of art she will push people off of ledges, seduce them into following their bliss. She always knew that making things was good for people. The monster will be fed every lovely person on the planet. In the name of art she will throw a party. In the name of art she will have a ball.

Sully

oh Sully

my dead cat Sully
who chased squirrels to
the ends of the roof

who mauled mice into
squeaky guts

who courted the kitten next door
with 2 dead robins
placed just so

who leapt from kitchen counter
to tabletop to chair to teevee

even falling fearlessly

who ate hard food when i
bought him soft

who suckled on my ears
until he was weaned
and even after

who when hit by a car
with ripped tail, broken ribs
clawed his way back to our porch
a lumpy mess by the screen door

suffering ignominiously
until i had the heart
to kill him.

oh Sully

shit.

Googleplex

We are both on our knees
looking for your lost contact lens
in the green thigh-high carpet.

Today your lips are larger than usual.
Your one eye closed, I feel like
a monster befriending a blind girl.

You invite me over for an evening of
coaxing kittens out of your cat,
and something in me inhales.

Your son sick, snot pulsing
in, out of his nose as he breathes—
battling colds in his sleep.

It took me time to grow into
my appetites; time for you
to grow up around your belly.

My heart's desire to wear a slinky
dress, festooned with boas, to your
prom in that golden garden.

I want you sodden and flagrant;
you and me against the skies
that ducks desire.

Our Rock-Star Year

Ryan busks outside the Rivoli
while I sing a tuneless tune.

The guitar case is open, ready
for business. Our big cardboard
sign says, "Help us get home."

People are stopping us all the
time, asking, "Where're you from?"

And I would answer Montréal, or
Kingston, or Ottawa—

anywhere I'd been long enough
to answer shallow questions about.

But one time this guy asked, and
I answered, and he offered

—said he was going there—

and that's how we
ended up here.

Undertow

*

we started imitating ourselves early,

throwing up a beautiful bastard's art
out of a satchelful of personas.

it looked like success when we
fell into the mirror.

**

they wanted to keep us and watch us
forever because we were sexy, sweet and nice.

they thought that they were doing it for love.
and so did we.

knowing nothing was more exciting
than a circle of outrage.

but like field mice, we never quite slept
awaking startled under the starry vaults.

we became rock and roll aristocrats.
old draculas

writing down phone numbers in the dust,
blaming everything on the bomb.

***

they saw us as old-fashioned farts
not dirty old men.

those kids that are wide open—
you could suck on them like licorice.

the long-lashed girl,
angry pout on her mouth.

the chord-savvy boy,
pirouetting on the side.

there were different versions of them
in every city.

detailing wishful fictions in
autographs and kisses,

alighting like monarch butterflies
at the after—party,

us offering them
only decaf and rum.

what we did they would dine out on
for the rest of their lives.

we set it up so that the only
conceivable relationship possible

would be to kiss us
or to kill us.

they knew what they were doing.
they were hoping to get caught.

Alice

3 a.m.
7-11
all trashmags
and teethrot
the cashier
all bruised and
battered for
show and tell
and finally
to look at her
without blinking
her name-tag on
her green jersey—
Alice

i have
lifted magazines
in my pockets
up my sleeve
and i am buying
something
insignificant
and she asks me
how i am and i tell
her and she tells
me a joke but the
punchline is always
lost in the ringing
of the cash and
the rustle of
my bag and the
closing of the door
behind me

That Jenny Girl

that jenny girl turns to me
and says, "last night i had gin
for the first time. woo!"
and i say to her, "was it good?"
and she turns to me and lowers
her voice, like someone could
actually overhear her at this
crazy party, and she says,
"gin. jesus. that's a *panty-*
removing drink." and i laugh.
"don't tempt me with that info,"
i tell her, "i'll abuse it."
and she tells me to "abuse *every-*
thing!" and i laugh again.
i pull some more cold beer
into my mouth and let the day's
strain bleed out of me. my job
makes me thirsty tonight. this
jenny girl is reminding me that
we all want to be weekend stars.
in our off-hours to come to close
approximations of constellations.
jenny's ice cubes clink in her
glass and i ask her, "what are
you drinking tonight?" and while
she sniffs her drink to remind
herself, i am thinking about how
making love makes everyone
a millionaire.

Subway

i like him.

makes the stupid hat, the
stupid shirt look good.

lays green peppers
in an odd shape on
my sandwich.

squirts mayonnaise.
peppers it,
and salts.

one eye up—
"anything else?" or
sometimes, 'that'll be all?'

i nod yes,
watching him
wrap it up.

when i go to give
my tip, he's not looking.
i like that too.

and i just knew how gentle
he'd be, closing the cash
register with all that
money in it.

The Going Price Of Shit

My brother stopped caring
about our mom one day.
Smatterofact, he walks
into the kitchen, and he's
this kid, all of ten,
saying to me, "I've
stopped caring for Mum."
I raise an eyebrow, moving
my spoon slowly through
the Fruit Loops. "Oh,
you have, have you?"
"Yup," he says.
"What brought this on?
This sudden change of
heart?" I ask, and
suddenly there are tears
in his eyes as he deadpans,
"It hurts too much to
give a shit. Don't give
a shit," he tells me.
"Don't ever give a shit!"
"Don't worry," I wink,
"I'm not just handing it
out or anything. You
have to pay."

School Trip To NYC

that dark bar
we ended up in.

the brunette at the
table beside us.

she said
it's my birthday today.
my husband usually beats
me but he didn't beat me
today.

you're college students,
aren't you? i went to
college for a year but
i had to drop out
because my husband
said he wouldn't pay
for it anymore.

she was in tears,
but wanted us to
celebrate with her.

The Best Things About Silas Meoko

* His red Raleigh bike named Plummet. My name is Laura Plummet. The capital of the state I live in is Raleigh. Obviously, it's fate that Silas Meoko and I were meant for each other. Obviously. That or his bike and I were meant for each other. But that is more disturbing (For me. Less so for him, I'm sure).

* I like the way he talks, in his ever-so-soft and seductive slightly broken English and Scottish lilt. If I was a girl I'd have a crush on him just because of the way he talks.

* I don't know Silas Meoko, but I said "hello" once.

* I think Silas would make a lovely best friend because he's sweet and soft-looking. He seems like the kind of boy who wears a scarf when it's cold outside. I'll bet he likes doing idle things like reading books and taking naps. I'd love to nap with him.

* All my friends think he sounds gay. And he doesn't, but I'm glad they think that, because it means I won't have to fight over him with them, like he was a member of some boy band or something. He can also lift really heavy things, which is useful.

* I like his eagerness to do his own stunts, even though they could just put a wooly hat on a scarecrow, and throw it over a cliff, and no one would know or anything.

* You get the feeling that he is a very considerate and compassion-ate human being. When I spoke to him at a *Heaven's Liable* gig I tried to get him to sign my HL T-shirt for me. What he said was, "Ach no, I can't." When I inquired why not, he said that it would get him "intae bother" because it was Isobel's band. So instead, he ran off to find her so she could sign it for me. I just think that was very sweet and thoughtful.

* I like Silas' pink felt pants, because they are funny, and they hug his little bum. You look at him and you just sense he could make love to you in a dewy field forever.

* I like Silas when he tries to talk over a megaphone and it is still quieter than most people's normal speaking voices, and everyone

has to strain and concentrate really hard to hear what he is saying. Because it is probably either witty, or silly, or helpful. When he forgets the lyrics to his songs, or rambles on about something no one can quite make out on stage, that is when I say, "Silas, you are the new rock and roll."

* I like Silas because he makes wonderful music that I can't stop listening to and never grow tired of. *And* he makes me end sentences with prepositions. *Naughty!*

* There are many lovely things about Silas. I met him about a month ago when Chloé and Jai did their DJ thang here in Toronto...some of the lovely things which I witnessed then were (1) His beautiful voice. (2) His good memory...he remembered me when I met him again. (3) His wonderful gorgeous dancing...he kinda hops about and waves his arms...ahhh (drool drool drool). (4) His lovely nature. He gave us free stickers and autographed my book. (5) His lovely nature once again...we told him we were standing right in front of him when he had his seizure and he was actually worried...

* I love Silas Meoko's songs because of the way he puts polaroids in his songs—little snapshots in a sentence or two that convey something more substantial than most pop songs—"'You jerk,' the sole honest thing you ever said to me, feeling shitty the sole honest thing I've ever done." And because of his rhyming ability—who else could think of "chocolate" and "talk shit" as rhymes, and pull them off?

* He makes me feel understood, more than any other singer ever could. It's best when he sings really high, like in "Hint of Citrus" and "Muddy Me."

* If I could ever meet Silas Meoko I'd ask him to make me a sandwich. I would let him pick out the ingredients because if he can make sandwiches like he can think up songs I don't think I'd ever have to eat again.

* I didn't like his hair when he dyed it ginger. I liked it best when it was black and all Beatley, like in the video "Soft-Boiled Boy."

* I had my fingers in Silas' mouth once. At a recent gig in Montréal, Silas had an epileptic seizure on stage. I took off my t-shirt and stuffed it into his mouth to keep him from biting his own tongue. I held his head until his feet stopped kicking.

* I like Silas' little dancey bit on stage. It's dead cool. Dread, as they say in England. I bet Silas is a secret rastaman. He is also the only person who can say "cell phone" and grant the words some semblance of dignity. Thinking of his face I feel peaceful.

* Silas' voice is soft and wispy and lispy and filled with quiet pathos, a true girly-man voice, and I mean that in the best possible manner, 'cos I *lurve* girly men.

* He writes great songs about girls. (And boys too, but that's not surprising being that he's a boy himself.)

* He sounds like he's totally bluffing his way through the modern world when he sings about "silicon chips," "dropping pills," and "marketing analysts."

* Can anyone here help? I heard he was once in a band called *The Devil's Advertiser,* and then *Hoity-Toity.* Is this true?

* I get a tingle down my spine when Silas says "lovers" in "Hipless Girl." It sounds like "law-fers." It makes my knees weak whenever I hear it, even still. See, before I knew he was such a hot item, I figured I would date him without having ever seen his face. All I wanted was for him to sing to me and write songs for me—selfish me— yet I didn't care what he looked like. And I knew that when the day came that I would finally see this elusive creature's face, that I would be smitten. I was right. Funnily enough though, I've yet to see him clearly in those band photos. He's always turning his head and blurring it. I suppose I'd be lucky if I even recognized him on the street.

Undressed

she was a date rape victim
for halloween, that year all
the seventh graders at her
school dressed up as strippers.
there was a rumour that her
father was once caught kissing
one of his daughters in a
photobooth at eaton's. she
was a girl whose teeth
weren't growing in right,
and who needed braces. the
flash glinted off her half-
opened mouth giving the girl
a smile of diamonds. and
while the dark brown curtain
was drawn, harmless pop
played over the airwaves.

New Kid

There was a new boy in the class. His name was Gail. We couldn't understand this. "You mean 'gale,' like wind?" I asked him. "No. Gail." he said. Then he spelled it. What's more, I heard from my mom that his mom's name was Peter. And that his dad's name was Eleanor. Of course we had to kill them.

Coming Clean

for Carolyn Smart and the
Queen's Creative Writing Class of 1998

I.

photocopy your heart
         and put it on the table

heaps of guts in a
                squishy buffet

i'll give you a spoon
with the piece.
          say, oh yes!
        i'm brilliant. Please.

II.

        hmm.

III.

you are pasting livers
beside the brains
        —wouldn't they look better
over *here?*

      —oh, are these
         your guts? sorry.

IV.

you offer up mouthfuls
               of yourself
for peoples' yesses
           & noses.

you are all beautiful full
        fucked-up lives

oh! i couldn't stop staring.

Dirty

I.

these are long days on your estate.
the crew and i have been at it for hours.

by the time you get home, i am a fetid, sweaty,
dirty man on a field of green.

your starched shirt is loose, your tie is gone.
you've rolled your kilt up like all the cool girls do.

i hoe, i dig, i mow, i clip. i am reduced to verbs here
landscaping in Westmount.

II.

your house is so clean that even my socks leave marks on the
carpet. your maid undoes all my work, two steps behind me.

there's a room i pass on my way to the bathroom
that looks like it's never been used. all these ornate
golden eggs beside framed photos, under shaded lamps.

i fantasize you want me to house-sit for the weekend.
feed the cat, water the plants, that sort of thing.
i'd draw myself a bath, with bubbles, and scrub myself clean.

III.

sometimes it's you who brings out the lemonade,
setting down the tray on the flatbed of the truck.

"one day," i joke, "i'm going to take you away from all this."
my tanned arm sweeps across trees, pool, Mercedes, house.

we share a cigarette, and you tell me it's
not all it's cracked up to be. you want to split.
you're thinking of going to boarding school. or California.
or boarding school in California.

you tell me about your mother standing naked on the
driveway, at 3 a.m., hollering after your father,
"go on then! go cheat on me again! why don't you just *go!*"

then you tell me about how your grandfather committed
suicide, drunk out of his mind, falling from the second
floor landing, right in front of your dad.

i choke on my lemonade.
"why are you *telling* me all of this?"

you just laugh, shake your head. "i don't know," you say
to me, dropping the cigarette on the lawn, smushing
it with your loafer. "my parents are cracked."

Springfield, America

In Springfield, Maine, I saw the fattest
man I'd ever seen watering his lawn at
night, in big blue star-spangled shorts.

In Springfield, New Hampshire, I found
a single-sheet suicide note marking a
dusty page in a library book.

In Springfield, Vermont, I threw a
penny into a pool at a mall, pitching
for more than a lukewarm life.

In Springfield, Massachusetts, I
looked up "teen suicide" on the
internet and got a porn site.

In New Canaan, Connecticut, I went to see
a movie about Jesus, where the popcorn was
His body, and the cream soda, His blood.

In Manhattan I walked along a rusted street,
by ashen ironwork, staring at lights, at
unreal indivisuals, downing a Coke.

In Springfield, New Jersey, I'd visited an amusement
park and met a woman named Clitora, her two
daughters Vulva and Labia, and her son Scrotum.

In Springfield, Pennsylvania, a cult tried
to recruit me with flowers and faith,
but I knew better than that.

In Springfield, West Virginia, I sat watching
Indiana Jones drink from the Holy Grail as I ate
my TV dinner of turkey, mashed potatoes and peas.

In Springfield, Virginia, I found a lost
collarless dog who asked me with its
eyes what happened to its humans.

In Springfield, South Carolina, I went to
a club that was like onions, so filled with
cigarette smoke it made me want to cry.

In Springfield, Georgia, I sat in a laundromat,
dryers hot as ovens, watching people fold their
clothes with the tenderness of nurses.

In Springfield, Florida, a boy laughed
as the waves pummelled his sand castle into
mud, again and again.

In Springfield, Alabama, facing each other
with rifles, the New Black Panthers
called the KKK "melanin-deprived."

In Springfield, Louisiana, I passed
a man on the street with this sign:
"Every beggar is Jesus in disguise."

In Springfield, Arkansas, I saw a
boy that looked like he was a girl.
Or he should've been.

In Springfield, Missouri, I dreamt I was a time
traveller who'd gotten caught up in an era and forgotten
that he was a time traveller; that he could leave.

In Springfield, Tennessee, I joined
in a search for a missing girl, but
we never found her body.

In Springfield, Indiana, I saw baby clothes
with art prints on them. Picasso's Blue period
was for boys, his Rose period, for girls.

In Springfield, Kentucky, the boys told
a girl that if she could touch her elbows
together behind her back, that that meant
that she was an angel. And she could.

In Springfield, Ohio, a lonely
man invented a hug machine,
making my arms obsolete.

In Springfield, Illinois, I went to an art
opening, paintings lined up against the
wall like prisoners waiting to be shot.

In Iowa, I visited the Field of Dreams
but didn't see anything out there.

In Springfield, Minnesota, I died in a car
accident, had a near-death experience, returned
to my body, and didn't have time to lie anymore.

In Springfield, South Dakota, I had
my palm read and she identified every
line except one.

In Springfield, Nebraska, someone tried
to sell me Girl Scout Condoms and I
suddenly realized how old I had become.

In Springfield, Colorado, I pissed in a
swimming pool, the still warm wet against
my skin, then cold again.

In Navajo, Arizona, I ran out of gas and
walked in the heat seeing a king before me
wearing a jester's hat for a crown.

In Springfield, Idaho, there were 33
dwarfed bunnies for sale beside a
wooden sign on the dusty road.

In Springfield, Oregon, I remembered my
mother in a field, her autumn skirt spread out
before her like a carpet, apples in the folds.

On the West Coast on a beach I was lying
on my back when an odd-looking cat
started suckling on my nipple.

Rich Bastard

he'd pee in
the corner behind
the teevee, drunk
out of his mind.
totally no respect
for his own house.

his dad
(on call 24/7)
the gynecologist,
always puttering
around, asking
us boys if we
wanted to see some
pictures that would,
in his words,
turn us off pussy
forever.
"no," we'd say.

and his mom, who
was a total bitch,
and no wonder,
neglected like
she was, always
looking at our
young bodies
through her
cigarette cloud,
telling her son
that maybe
we'd like
something
to drink.

Smooches

the new cat.
kitten really.
a little slip
of a cat.

lifting her up
like a ball in
one hand, trusts
the touch of skin
on paw.

she's cute;
knows it too.
maybe not.

isn't yet old enough
to refuse to walk
on a leash.

i take her to
the park at 4 p.m.:
falling apart, crowds
of kilted schoolgirls
want to touch her, hold
her, stroke her—
with a freeness reserved
only for cats, babies,
boyfriends.

I Blankety-Blank You

i was taken
by surprise

you were two arms
receiving me

and i remained calm

like a quieted cat
no panic, no nothing

even a little purring

and we had a drink

in your cupboard
always something
to sing me to sleep

against each other
without covers

by now you are in
your bathroom, rubbing
your eyes, picking
your nose, massaging
your teeth, toes curled
on the cold tiles
like exposed animals

and i am in my bathroom
held up by the tub's water
pubic hair a wet nest
cold knees like mountaintops
and i am slumbering under
the weight of another winter
wondering whether to wake up
or to let go

I Know You Are But What Am I

you tell me that this temporary arrangement between friends is a perfect idea not only for the reasons we'd outlined, but for other benefits not yet known.

you play your madcap piano tunes, upsweep holy hair into your headband, cram thirteen cans of frozen orange juice into your freezer, walk down the twisted corridors of your apartment in your mom's sexy sixties high-heeled boots.

you tell me about your friend who collects children's shoes on the beach in the summer, and lost mittens in the winter. you finger paint lovely touching portraits you refuse to admit are of yourself. you hang sheets like tents around your room. you love tom waits as if his voice came from your lungs. and your breath in my ear is driving me crazy.

when i try to figure out what we are, you tell me that that sort of thing isn't important to you. you'd prefer we didn't pin ourselves down. you tell me that my need to, is not something that you'd like to do.

you tell me you're more comfortable not being sure. you tell me that we are different people. you tell me that it wasn't supposed to be like this. that you are not in love.

Falling Apples

used to smack bloody lips in mirrors
        practising for fame

stunning glimmer gel and candy-coated
        glazes seal my nest
        of glossy pages

oh jesus
        i'd be on my knees by the bed
        hands clasped like bodies
        come together

make me a star
        take me up that tunnel so i can
        sing songs like adolescent drawings

so my mom will watch me on teevee, see
        me in magazines full of girls
        soaking in their squishy clothes,
        tiara crowns turning them into suns

satin slips line the walls, chiffon dresses
        hang from nails

pink panties sheathe the bulb
        turning my room warm

i am a girl in braces
        with pleading eyes—
        i'll be pretty soon

all too aware of the blue haze
        in spackly white sitcom kitchens

probably inappropriate
        but trying to convince me otherwise

knowing, in an eleanor rigby world
        with edie sedgwick eyes, i am
        grinning all sudsy and frothy
        and empty as soap operas

knowing, i am standing knee-deep in snow
        and need shoes

        did you know that there are
gurls who spend all high skule
learning to keep their knees together,
        then waiting for university to
        learn how to fly?

        and did you know that frying
sausages look like penises sheathed
in milky condoms?

        and i had the spit
all ready in my mouth because
did you know that in cannibal
societies it's taboo to eat someone
from your immediate family?

        knowing that
sometimes we break our
shells & unfold like a cardboard box

        & knowing, that sometimes
stage crew boys all across america
spotlight the loves of their lives
& read dickens & jane austen books
in their closets under a tender bulb

        all of this
ending in comedy
rather than tragedy

Avant-Garder Than Thou

I was at
this art show.

Okay, I thought. That
painting's pretty okay.
But I dunno. It's kind
of pretentious.

It felt like all
the canvasses where
screaming, "I am the
real fucking deal."

I looked around.
That's crap, I thought.
I mean, holy shit.
It's shit.

I glanced over at the girl
who had painted them.
She's cute, I thought.

I took another look
at the paintings.

Puss In Boots

Janice, eating her
honest french fries, her brand new
boots resting on the table.
I am giving advice again, mumbling
something about McLuhan.
Her feet fall to the floor.
She says that I should drop it.
I'm silent, knowing she's
agonized over clothes that don't quite
cover up her marks, though I've run my
fingers over her scars like Braille,
though I've caught her twice with the
silver scissors she keeps in her bag.

Later, I am offered
bellies, throats. Watch as they
swallow, heave. I stroke the
backs of her mangled knees
like bunnies.

She tells me she gets tired of
wanting people to like her. Says that
she spends too long convincing herself
that her fascist father really knows
what's best for her, convincing herself
that all she feels are nothing but
chemical twitches.
My family is so angry, she says.
I've seen them, huddled like crows in front
of the TV, waiting for something to be run over.
I go to the kitchen and bring her some
yogurt, and myself a bottle of ginger beer.
Did you know that America stopped
singing? she asked. America is her
frog. She named her frog America.

Janice mews in her sleep,
and grinds her teeth, and I watch her
lips moving, puckering, pursing
coaxing herself back
to calmness.

Retire Tomorrow

That's tonight's deal: naked breasts, bum, scent of lilied underbelly, hot body. Tomorrow night no naked—nothing. I had a forecast about this not-too-distant future.

I never pretended to aspire to more than a one-hit wonder, to making it big and hosting legendary parties. This game involved burping books out, generating buzz, and pretending you had more going on than the endless everydayness of it.

When you're famous you radically increase the percentage of girls who'll readily sleep with you, and my poems target-marketed a particular kind of girl who'd go for me.

I loved that book because it was my first one and it let me sleep in and eat out and live large for the next ten years. My first and last hit—people still know me for it.

I generated a buffer of beautiful people between me and reality. Being famous would be my redemption from ugliness. My wrinkles and cracks soon came to indicate character.

Fame is an interesting medium. It's the closest to an afterlife I'd get. Marinating myself in love-juice I became calm and unruffled—my skin unlined. I went through groupies the way a summer fire eats through dry grass.

The beginning of my fame fetish can be positively linked to a single incident that occured during my pre-adolescent years. 60 years later, the memory remains vivid, the effect profound.

I looked toward the sunset-hued umbrella drinks on that forty-footer on the waves. My friends and I were famous to each other—big nobodies with bruised and naked toes.

I came from a long line of mindfuckers, adept as Bugs Bunny in lipstick and flowers, chomping on carrots, puckering those lips.

Every connection opens you up to being conned, but we offered up illusions, and you were consenting adults. Let me remind you that this was your arranged marriage to a supermodel, and that the only true reason to become famous is to not to have to hire hookers one day.

I gathered all my poems together and told them that we were travelling to a better place, a land of opportunity. Not until they were on the tracks and across the border did they realize they were being sold.

In the not-too-distant future, a book emerged. Nothing sacred escaped unscathed. With all the cartoon variety violence, the silly treatment of profound issues, the cynical wit, brash and clever, even the President's Daughter, who systematically seduced every boy at her private school, liked it.

A banned book had a certain cachet, and the resulting controversy provided a platform for publicity. Some of my students found the book offensive. "Only out of respect, because he was our teacher, did we not beat him to death on the spot," said Zoë Smith, 17. Shortly thereafter, a shipload of books was overturned into the ocean, becoming unglued.

"I can't say why I continue to gamble," I told the press. "You feel you have to somehow get the love lost back." And as for not having a steady job? "Don't wolves live from kill to kill? They keep lean and fierce that way. Travel in packs. I think it's true that god loves the hungry, otherwise we'd never have made it this far." Our talent-sodden crew committed regrettable acts of self-defence. Our small-run books offered shelter from the barrage of compulsory happiness.

We didn't need to, but we did. The factory practically ran itself. My name was on top of taxis. I decided to branch out into films, art, entropy. Breakdown was always a blue-chip stock. Blank aspirations filled by the book where all this trouble began.

Meteor Shower

even bringing you tea strikes me as funny

hilarious as the sun smiling behind those far bushes
by the swamp that backs onto your yard

the torches that were supposed
to keep the bugs away didn't work

the flies are dark clouds in the orange air,
like motorcycle gangs

lying on your roof with you on a cold night, looking
over at the satellite dish, then at the stars

a meteor shower bathing us,
your eye always catching ones i didn't see

your face a cool rising moon on the rough black roof
beside mine

me stuck with itches to scratch all night

your succulent aloe plants
drooping with all their juice

thank you for crushing those leaves,
smoothing the cooling fluid over my spots

big aching bumps

you must've thought i was doing something,
moving underneath my rocket-ship sheets

scratch, scratch

Afterschool Specials

You were my best friend, a boy they called a "fringe element." The first time we met you said to me, "Ha! You think you're invisible, but I see you." We started hanging out. You confided in me that you were one of four in a national network of terrorist sleeper cells, to be activated at any time by the leader, a small man with a big head in a foreign country.

In our spare time we were superheroes. We fought evil afterschool. Our clubhouse was my walk-in closet, and you were my sidekick. Boutique Réalité we called it. We'd huddle under dresses and overcoats, and the first thing I did was to pick out your costume. I decided on a blue blanket as a cape, and some star-spangled panties for a bottom. You protested, but I would hear none of it. Brand image was important.

Some days we would try on each other's costumes. You looked cute in my tight leopard-print catsuit. You tried to change out of it, but I held you by the tail. You nearly slipped free, but I held tight. "Don't worry," I told you. "Your secret's safe with me." I had a suitcase with a kit in it: everything that would go on my utility belt once I'd finally crafted it. I was ready for any eventuality, no matter where we'd have to go.

Under that low light I'd bounce from corner to corner, sliding in and out of rows of clothes. I'd appear as Avant-Garde Girl, Quite-Nice Woman, and Ms. Rather-Pleasant-Person. I'd utter my special word and transform. In my real-life alternate identity I was never this beautiful. My legs would lengthen and my breasts would get bigger. Objects would fly from the walls, flung to the other side of the bed. A supernatural glow would suffuse everything. And I changed the same way every time, knowing that only strict adherence to the time-honoured tradition would bring about the magic. I wasn't afraid to be larger than life. I had absolute faith in it, like a hoax I knew I could pull off. I knew that you would believe, so I believed. I stayed in the air, held up only by the public's astounded gaze. A second's disbelief and I'd be dead.

My superpower was to create mini black holes I could dive into, and pull in after myself. I slid through those self-created wormholes like sheath-dresses. I'd always reappear at home, 2 inches above my bed. Then I'd pull you through, plucked from certain death. Then into the closet to change for breakfast. We'd emerge in PJs and slippers, rubbing our eyes with the knuckles of our sore fists.

Over a year we'd saved hundreds from spousal abusers, thousands from sexual assault, millions from murder, billions from bombs, kazillions from machete headhunters. It's unrealistic in the aggregate, but it happens every day. The job however, of keeping us from throttling over the brink of our own extinction became less and less fulfilling. As a regularly appearing character, one of the things that happened was that my ability to do anything else but what I was, diminished with every episode. I talked to you about quitting, though by now entire economic ecosystems depended on our continued fight. We didn't just save lives, we were franchised. I didn't know if I could pull the plug on what we had become. At night you'd sleep with me on my bed, exhausted. You curled like a croissant.

A Little Over A Year In Montréal

The woman with the well-stocked closet
is recklessly emptying it—flinging
skirt after shirt after chemise over
the bed to land on the other side.

Relaxed, they gather
like guests at a party.

Everything matches.

Bedtimers

for isabelle

we have both
taken some of
that medication
that comes powdery
in little packets,
sweet and lemony.
and we are both in
bed, writing things.
the cat is asleep
at our feet, safe
and full of love
for us, but in a
casual way, and i
can feel us falling
as i lie here, back
propped up on pillows,
the light getting
warmer, your skin
getting softer, every
line disappearing
under every other
line, and i am for the
first time thinking
about how nice it
would be to grow old
and incoherent
together,

mumbling
ourselves
asleep.

She Would

paul was lamenting about some band.

"it's sad when they get more polished. when
they get more money they don't sound better."

i wasn't really listening. i was thinking of this
girl. we were definitely physical, sort of.

we were at this loft party and the lineup for the
only bathroom was super long. we had gotten to
talking, and we were both drunk.

i went at the sink and she went at the toilet.
she just peed in the bathroom with me. easy.
afterwards we kept talking, and everything was cool.

people who don't have any assumptions about things.
it's a weird kind of freedom to hang around them.

paul's not like that. i mean, sure, he's got
all the usual vices—flirting with his girlfriend's
best friend, for example, that sort of thing.
but he'd never seduce her sister.

something about this girl would.

What I Did After My Housemate Was Killed And Before His Parents Had Time To Fly To Montréal

i looked in his room, of course,
in his pockets, in the drawers,
looking for things i thought a
dead man might not need anymore.
because life feeds on life,
you know, and all of that.
and i found a large Pepsi bottle,
filled with change. i remember
we used to steal change from
the laundry. there was one
machine, and i guess they lost
the key or something, but they
used to keep the change box locked
with a bike lock. they'd punched
holes in the sides of the white
steel, and closed it up with the
lock. but we'd pull it out as far
as it could go, and he'd get out
the double-sided tape and we'd
go at it, pulling out loonies and
quarters, 50, sometimes 60
dollars. and this bottle was full
of that. and he had money on the
bedside table, and stamps, and all
of that went into my pocket.
and the porn he kept nearby,
that was mine, though i thought
about leaving it for his parents
to find, to show that he was a real
person, no use censoring the dead.
i left the condom packages, so that
they'd know he was getting laid
regular, you know, but i kindly
grabbed a handful of tissue and
picked up the used condoms he was
too lazy or too tired to trash.
so this is what i did.
life feeds on life, and
all that, you know.

Six Lies About The Group Of Seven

1.

Sometimes when Frederick Varley
was taking a shit, he would imagine,
when the stool was halfway out,
halfway in, halfway hanging between
the clouds of his asscheeks and
the placid lake below, that maybe
that was what it would be like
to be fucked up the ass, like
Zeus with a bolt of lightning.

2.

A.Y. Jackson, first sketching
with Tom Thomson in Algonquin Park,
pouring dirty turps into a nest of
needles by the green pine tree he'd
just painted, cleaning brushes with
a shirt and some soap, skinny-dipping off
a sun-warmed rock, Tom up on the slope,
pretending not to notice, wondering
at times, where it all came from,
and where it all went.

3.

Arthur Lismer taking a mid-afternoon
nap at work, dreaming of his fourth-grade
teacher dressed in a muffin costume
saying to him, "Eat me, I'm moist,"
and finally emerging bothered and
bleary-eyed from the Ontario College of Art,
buttoning up his coat and stepping down
onto McCaul, marvelling at the colour
in a passing woman's cheeks.

4.

J.E.H. MacDonald, with Morrice
and Matisse in Tangiers, watching
horny, in a tight, cramped room,
circle of chairs surrounding
the weeping stained mattress,
the couple fucking on the floor,
the smell of their sex seeping
into clothes, facial hair,
MacDonald's paint-smeared hands
aching to stop the furious
twirling of her red-pearled tit.

5.

Frank Johnston and Franklin
Carmichael, one night high on the
fumes of paint and turpentine,
buy a nickel's worth of gasoline,
and float like ghosts down to
the lake, buying tobacco from
a shop along the way, and in
a moment of lucidity, Frank
keeping Franklin from blowing
them both up.

6.

Lawren Harris brushing past
blue-blazered boys at Trinity
College School, them gazing after
their art teacher, him still shaken
from the night before, having watched
a bloody bar fight where a man was
stabbed and his guts fell out, Harris
playing dead in a corner, hungry
for the open air, that night having
the best sex he'd ever had with
his girlfriend of seven months.

Bitter Girl Chronicles

"Nothing happened
that I didn't expect,
and that is part of the
problem," she says—
"always a good friend
and never a girlfriend."

The boy she likes,
the boy who is her friend,
never seems to find her shaking
her sweatered arms, swaying
in her ankle-length skirt
DJing unofficially at a party.

She doesn't want to play
the giggle game, furious with
batting lashes, ingratiating grins.
Drives her nuts to see her
sister accommodating so many men
so well.

"God, I want to get laid,"
she murmurs, "get one of
those boyfriends you can take
someplace, have a few drinks,
a few laughs, catch a cab
and take home."

Tiptoe To Thunder Bay

Ryan told me it would
take 28 hours by bus
to creep along the Lake
Superior shoreline, to crawl
up its ragged back toward
his hometown Thunder Bay.

They stop in every town,
he tells me, to shit, to eat,
to unwind long legs like
carpets, only to be rolled up
again and kept crammed against
the pressure of someone
else's back.

I imagine the highway is a
winding rope the driver rolls
between her fingers, tying a knot
at every diner, truck stop and
gas station. Every hour in that
box polishing our patience
to a fine insanity.

Leaving after mid-terms, I'll
be helping celebrate other peoples'
Christmasses, helping to string
tinsel and hang lights on
grateful green trees. Dinners
in houses stranded by winter,
full of the walking unsaid.

Seeing my friend among his family
I wonder if he'll be more or less
himself. Better not give him
the time to anticipate all this.
We should fly.

Cooking Lessons

Kristen, tall skinny blonde,
Miss Nanaimo 1992, was helping me
cook french fries for the first time.
"Keep it at medium for the first bit,"
she said, "but if the oil starts
smoking, turn it down."

"Okay," I said, holding vigil over
the stove. After awhile, when the oil was
manic in the pan, she suggested,
"Put your finger in there."
I almost did, I was so intent on
following her instructions.

Levelling my eyes at her,
I said, very carefully,
"Now, why did you tell me to do that?"
"Because I'm my father's daughter."
she replied. I stared at her for a moment.
Somewhere I missed something.

Tack Shoppe

There's a store
in downtown Kingston
that sells riding helmets,
breeches and boots for
blonde girls who have ponies.

There's another store for
            prom dresses.

All these clothes you'll grow into.

They come across in monotone.
I hear them in stereotypes.

I wonder how automatic acceptance
affects their equally complex lives.
I see them seeing immensity
in their shiny eyes.

Situation Normal: All Frocked-Up

my feet are still aching 2 days later, with tiny little blisters on 2 of my toes. the ones beside the littlest ones, skin rubbed off all soft and raw. i am *still* walking funny.

i was a prom girl on halloween. size 10 pumps from the bargain bin at the *le château* entrepôt. slinky silky black dress from the Rue St. Catherine street sale. bargains both.

a bunch of us met up at jenny's to get dressed and get made up and to tag temporary tattoos on each other. i was in the too-bright washroom, stuffing dress-pads into my pantyhose, trying to develop some hips and a bum.

i'd scraped hard at my facial stubble, my armpits stinging from their virgin shave, my legs featureless as hard-boiled eggs. i was a crusty newborn, dabbing honey-coloured cover-up on the grey haze over my lips.

mascara gunking on my non-existent lashes, like morning eye-crust all the time. each blink gluing together, i wipe the black stuff off.

finally to slip on the psychotic shoes, the dress coming down like a transporter beam, the bra stuffed, the wig on, the velvet gloves hugging my suddenly tender biceps like koalas on Australian trees.

i thought i was pretty sexy, but most boys say that. i stepped out of that bathroom unsteady, unready, and had to have a tequila to help prop me up. my friends, bless them, told me i looked great. karen poured me another drink. i smacked my lipsticked mouth and smiled.

we left for the party after sheridan arrived and all the tequila had disappeared. we were something out of the *justice league of america* going down that elevator.

the party was a dud. it failed to explode.

later on that drunken night, staggering up *de la montagne*, my purse dangling from my puppet-stringed arm, my hair in my face, my feet on fire, i said to myself, c'mon motherfucker, these shoes don't hurt, be a man.

It's Important To Hold Onto Someone
So You're Not Flung Off The Planet

for margaux and joe

he'd been clawing at the window for days.

saw the little kitten he liked—
tiny orangey-whitish ball—
begged the 2 girls who took care
of her to let him in.

finally they'd opened up—
let him see her.

joe, who used to live on the streets,
treated her gently as he could.

he used to kill things for her.
bring her half-maimed tiny strugglies
in the embrace of his mouth.

he used to go over there a lot.

one day he ambled over to
her place, scratched at the
basement apartment window screen
until they let him in.

but she wasn't there.
so they went looking for her.

over on the next street they
found her quiet and lying
one paw over the other
eyes open to nowhere.

joe went over to her, sniffing.

he turned and looked up and around
at the 2 girls staring, pleading,

someone get her off the street.

Pressed

She leans her pale
forehead against the glass
           but won't let you in—
           someone else is in there.

You almost pass out
                   on the road.

           Your head in
           your hands
           you blot out the moon.

           You have tried to
closet away these feelings,
put them away like toys.
           But somehow emotion
                   insists itself,
and presses like a crowded room
           on a closed door.

           You curl up
by a bush and cover
           your eyes.
                   You rock
     yourself into a deep
           prayer,
                   rocking yourself
           and rocking yourself,
until the prayer
           is praying you.

And left with an
           open palm of pain,
some keening
     quiet clarity,

           you know
           you are now
just another boy
           trying
     to seduce her.

Open

that sunday morning
after the night before
he played me a song
i could cry to, brought
me to his chest and let
me weep myself dry.

today, this sunny day,
ask yourself if you are
ready to break open,
and live the rest of
your life always on
the verge of tears.

SECRET 1

i broke up with my girlfriend &
i'm not even completely sure why we
broke up except that something had
become untenable about it in my head
that i wanted the relationship to end
& so i called her a nasty name
& that ended it.

SECRET 9

she liked to be tied up
& i liked to wear slips and stockings
& usually we're both terribly repressed people
who do very appropriate things appropriately
& that's probably why we found
each other in the first place &
why we stayed together so long
& i really didn't mind tying her up
& she thought i looked cute in the slip
but life is different now.

Whites

it seems like
they breed blondes
to wear & wash
white panties at
the laundromat

to pile their
filmy bras overtop
& tiny white tees
folded underneath

& let it sit in the
fluorescent lighting
like a belly wide open
for surgery

i do not dare
to steal a pair

it could get me in
a lot of trouble

she and her boyfriend
(i know for i saw him
kiss her)
are sitting around
the corner at
the next table

& i know they are
watching me

i just know they
are watching me

HERA HELP ME SAVE THE DAY,
LEST ALL EARTHS PERISH!!!

Ohmigod. These are just *so* much more comfortable. Suffering Sappho, those high-heeled motherfuckers were just *killing* me. Now I can fight crime like I was destined to. And me, a working girl in a Superman's world, I have to work *twice* as hard to get the same sorta respect. Though I'm happy for these boots. By *Aphrodite,* it was so embarassing when I was chasing after Dr. Psycho down the dark corridors of his secret hideout and my heel broke. I actually had to *stop* and try to take those skintight vinyl suckers off, but they were totally plastered on. It's like my sweat was *glue* or something. It's something similar to when I sat down on the Martian Manhunter's leather couch on that crazy hot day. *Fuck.* Lex Luthor was trying to melt the polar ice caps—*again.* But I was just *attached* to that couch. I swear it was like waxing my legs or something, it hurt *so much* peeling myself up. Anyway, taking those boots off took like, *forever.* The good Doctor even had time to stop and gloat. I can still hear the monster now: *Struggle, Amazon—Yes! Struggle in vain!! You have failed! Your world is mine!* Confident little fucker. Great Hera, it was so satisfying to truss him up in my golden lasso and make him tell, on tape, the truth about his dad and that awful "cattle prod" incident. But it kind of made me feel sorry for him, all the same. Just a bit. Though, hmm...he *was* trying to take over the world. Global domination, destruction of the known universe, yadda yadda yadda. Hmm. Speaking of global domination, wasn't I supposed to have a coffee at *Starbucks* this week with Hawkgirl? I know I wrote her beeper number down in my planner, but I think I left it in the invisible jet, and I can't remember where I parked it. Geez. You'd think Kal-El would be able to find it with that insane vision of his, but I guess he's still pouting, or a little embarrassed over last Saturday night. I mean, how in *Hera's Realm* was I supposed to know he didn't have...umm. You know. He was like a Ken doll or something. So I laughed. Wouldn't *you?* Some *Superman.* Shit. But look who's talking, I guess. My social life *is* the Justice League. Hmm. The Flash was looking pretty hot the other day. But he's probably a wham-bam kind of guy. Steve's probably hanging out with some army base skank, I just *know* it. Hmm. I wonder what Hawkgirl is doing tonight. Mmm. Those wings of hers. So *soft.*

Cheeks

They had ripped
his shirt off and
cut it into about
a million tiny pieces.

Then they sold all
the postage-stamp sized
squares alongside a
glossy photo of him.

Squares slightly
stained were worth
exponentially more.

Then they ripped him
apart, cooked him up
and packaged little Paul
McCartney beef boullion
cubes out of him.

On the box was a picture
of him in his early days
with the Beatles,
when he was a mop-top,
with his chipmunk cheeks.

London was mad for it.

Reassurance

oh daddy
of course I can
      take over the business.

I'm such a handsome lad,
      of course I can
      get the girls.

'course I can save
      the world.

nail me to that cross.

A Bad Day For Cats Named Chloé

I tried to kill myself again last night, but I just
wouldn't die. I felt like the cat who came back, or
one of those movie zombies, brought back from the dead,
empty arms outstretched, waiting to be filled.
And now here I am, missing your skintight love,
and it was something I wanted, but couldn't tell you,
that the heartbreakingly ugly eat their young.
Take my cat for instance, who eats her kittens like
dumplings, while they're still blind, stillborn,
fur slick and wet. Eats till her belly's full and
it's like she's pregnant again, meowing out her furry bum.
Of course I wanted my life filled with beauty and bliss,
the usual shit. But I've got feet like my mother's.
My toes are little pigs, mewling their way into the
starry world, wanting to be loved into life, instead
of kicked into being. Our tiny hands hug them kicking
and crying. Kittens climbing up my pant leg and
favourite sweater like squirrels up brown trees.
I wish I were a feral girl, able to swallow their
fear, have it beating in my chest like a current.
The priests have come to bring me to christ, to
fit me in a dress, sit me at a table, eat me with
a spoon. My head reeling with every expectation,
the sheer terror of asking for what you really want.
When you've grown old and grow up hungry and unfed,
the heartbreakingly ugly eat the gun.
And I am smart enough to know that I am in trouble.
All along there were limits to my largesse.
I'd spare myself some change, but I'd never, like, get
involved in a messy relationship with myself. I'd
saved all my affection for my cat. Enough love to
cover the moon. She tells me that it's okay for me
not to trust white people sometimes. The abused
abuser flogging himself because it is monday and I
am hugging suicide like a teddy bear again.

After Lunch, She Plays In Mud

The girls are all muddy.
They're all the same girl named Isabelle.
It's all the same mud covering her, smearing the walls.

She feels a little crazy like this. The mud could be a cleansing revivifying hydrating mask. It could be pie filling. It could be from mud wrestling. She is an afterschool special survivor. She loves to paint with mud, smeared like shit, like warm chocolate. Slick and sticky all over her hands, clothes, ears and hair.

Warm in the mud, she feels safe enough to see monsters, write bad words on the white tiles. She is drawing stories and wiping them out, each revision seeking an ending where she doesn't die. Every claw is sunk deep into the situation. She is wondering how long you can keep flushing a problem before it overflows, before it backs up and starts to stink. If she were hit by a car and flung into the air you would have only a fleeting glimpse of her beautiful desperation.

She is the girl working behind the make-up counter at Pharmaprix. The girl on the end of the line when you call to complain about your VISA statement. She is invisible. She knows what everyone is doing. She knows what everyone is saying. She can see their thoughts floating above them as if written on trailing balloons. She knows that the people themselves cannot read them. And she will not pop them, though she could. Even though one said, "Someone please stop me before I kill myself." She can't read her own usually. Only in a mirror.

Once the mud starts flowing, it will not stop until she is completely engulfed in it, nostrils full of the stuff. Her fluffy scarf is like a bubble bath keeping her head above water, her nose finding air. She is a science friction action hero keeping one step ahead of collapse, one sector in front of the blast.

She is a mile of mud stretched over millions in a fashion spread. She is bursting in, all out of breath and dripping, mud glistening, chest heaving. She looks like she just crawled out of a mudslide in Venezuela. She looks like she could go on forever. She looks like she just saved us all.

And they brought her in here and lit her up all nice,
and under the wind machine she feels right at home
looking for relatives in the maelstrom.

Devilishly Smooth Imposter

I swear to god I got into this for purely mercenary reasons.

After I became a cult superstar I made a habit of meeting every one of my female fans. I answered every letter with a date. White girls with blue hair all across the country invited me over for dinner. All the unconventional beauties I could ask for. They're really the best, those who can listen to the same album over and over again without getting sick of it. "You can sleep in my room," she said to me that time, taking my things.

Like Han Solo, I was after babes and cash. Figuring that somewhere along the line, I would end up saving the universe anyway. Isn't that the way things work out? I had that mix of rakish arrogance that closed deals, charmed girls, and brought the curtain down.

We all grew up fans, waiting for our place in the long line of succession in this devotional pyramid scheme. Early on we'd shape our lives like budding David Bowies. Everything we spoke was set in quotes, superimposed over flattering pictures. Another brick in the myth.

The first thing I saw when I walked into her room was a framed picture of me hanging on her wall. The frame was covered in black mohair. Another one had pink velour running around it. They reminded me of those furry toilet lid covers. The pictures were blowups of snapshots taken at one of my smaller readings. I remembered that one. I didn't remember her. "It's like you're saying everything I think," she told me. "I really connect with you."

They'd all want to know the same things, asking me the same questions. "Did all those things you wrote about really happen? What are your influences? Would you read some of my poems? What are you doing now?" And I'd think, "You. I'm doing you." And I would dream their clothes off.

"Sometimes I get depressed," she said. "And when I get depressed, all I want to do is sit in my room, turn down the lights, and listen to your music all evening." She was hugging her pillow, blinking out at me through her honey-coloured hair. "Me too," I laughed. "I make my way into the shower, and then I sing into the nozzle. I nearly drown." She rewarded me with a smile for this.

"You make suicide sound so good," she gushed. "It makes me want to do it." Her words hung in the air like bullets. I replied, "I mean, it's so catchy, I can't help but hum along with it. One person starts singing it, and pretty soon everybody's doing it. They can't get that tune out of their heads. Somebody got too good at their job." She'd collected everything that has to do with me. She even had the official unauthorized collector's edition of something I'd never even heard of. Bootlegs of readings. Old things I hadn't seen in years, stuff even I didn't have copies of anymore lined her shelves. They were like lost limbs I'd forgotten the feel of. When I told her this, she went, "Oh, do you want it? You should have it," she said. She pressed something into my hands, like returning a salmon to a stream. "Actually," I smiled, "I'm here to make a donation."

"Success kills your work," I gazed at the old books in my hands. "You get caught up in it. The pressure to follow up becomes unbearable. I'm probably going to fake my death, watch the prices on my pieces skyrocket, see the tribute albums emerge and retire early, before my work is killed by success, or overplay. And maybe I'll come back as someone else. It wasn't always me writing those songs. It was a persona that I'd adopt, take on. It all started out as a bit of a joke, really. A bit of a lark, this cult-hero con artist business. I was pretending the whole time, being someone who terrified me. It's like I married the bullies who used to beat me up afterschool, gave them my paycheques. Now I have sex with them. That's who wrote those songs. Blame my evil twin."

Eventually I'd started to feel like a broken record. They'd ask me to recite some poems and I'd be a jukebox firing off my greatest hits. But I'd do it with a smile. Sometimes I was a bank. People gave me this intangible thing, but with it I could manifest changes, cause riots, turn tides. I lay back while she put one arm around my neck and extended the other in front of us, taking a picture. The flash always stunned me. I made an effort to grin. "So are you seeing anyone right now?" I looked over and raised one eyebrow and she would blush and look at her bedspread that suddenly seemed unbelievably cheesy to her. "Nah. How about you?" and I'd tell her, "I guess I'm dating myself."

She showed me some excerpts from a notebook of mine, stolen from a reading I did two years ago. "It's on someone's Web site," she said. It had been in my bag, in the changeroom I'd been given to prepare in. Also missing were some nondescript boxers. A pubic hair retrieved from them, presumably mine, had been scanned and posted. It looked like mine but I couldn't be sure. Someone had animated it, making it flicker and twitch, and overlaid a recording of me reading, then singing. It screened in some small art film festival in Toronto.

I would sometimes talk about rebellion, falling on the subject seemingly by accident. It got girls wet. "It was all part of a fearless fuck-you," I said. I was suddenly on. "We were tired," I said. "We wanted no more hoity-toity posh toffs telling us to behave. 'Go fuck yourselves,' we said. We feasted on the hands that fed us," I told her, my eyes angling into her eyes. And then I slid her fingers into my mouth.

"When I started all this, I wanted to make a difference," my words mumbled around her skinny fingers. "I thought that I could help people, not add to the rabble of greedy children we all had become. But something happened. Along the way, leopard-print pants and sexy girls overwhelmed me like a tidal wave. I had been a lonely kid who wrote to feel better about himself, and who did readings to get some of the affection he never felt he got enough of. Then I sang and recorded flashy albums to make it all better. That's all any of this ever meant. I spread out into the world and then I ate it and felt full." Her fingers began to wrinkle, and I moved my tongue along the ridges. "I was trying to impress you." Her fingers explored my mouth, the crenellations of my molars, the ticklish scudded roof, my purring tongue. "When I was little," I told her. "I used to crawl all around. We went to malls. I had free reign. I embraced everything I could, and I could because I was a kid. I used to grab the breasts of my mother's friends. I looked up skirts as if at god." I made a hard wish, then closed my eyes. "Did you ever read Klaus Kinski's autobiography? It's called, *Everything I Do I Do for Love*. That's exactly how I feel." She delved deeper, aiming for the seat of my tongue. "Sometimes," I said, "I'm not who I believed myself to be. I'm trying less, these days, to be perfect, and more myself. I've become more forgiving."

She gave me this concerned look. "You're not feeling yourself?" she asked. "Look, I'm sorry." I replied. "I'm actually a little out of it." Maybe you'd like to lie down, I thought I heard her say. My parents are at a party. They'll be back later on tonight. And with that I dropped off her bed and onto the floor and into the ground beneath her house.

In the morning I was her. When I woke up I looked down at my small body and painted toenails and giggled. I spent the day as her. It was like she was asleep inside me, and I would have to shush her, stroke her hair like kittens, back asleep. The first thing I did was feel myself up in the shower, then I had breakfast with Mom and Dad. I, me, mine.

Later on I left the house and took a walk. A woman walked past me with a dog, who sniffed me. I thought about throwing myself in front of a truck, or off a bridge. Then I'd come back as myself, I thought. Tiring business, this.

Art Director's Note

Ads kill me. I come upon them like an accident scene. Late Capitalism is insane and I'm scared. I mirror it like a chameleon. I see televisually. We have to dive right in. Words are magic. The image is made flesh. This is an endgame deal. This is 2000. Nothing's normal anymore. Appearances eat us. You are what you simulate so be careful what you pretend. We have to approach the millennium with the guile of a psychopath. So don't run.

100 Views of
The Hokusai Wave

)   The Swell

1. always wanted to.
    a real bunny suit with ears.
    what would mother say?

2. my leg asleep.
    full of sand
    sparkling.

3. have to feed my cat.
    pour the kibble in the bowl.
    crunches away there.

4. we all wanted
    to be unconventional
    and uncool.

5. making a mixed
    tape full of love
    for her friend.

6. she's artsy-looking
    but not like she
    doesn't bathe.

7. they like to send
    people things here
    which is so nice.

8. a good-looking boy.
    saw him at a party once.
    paws girls like a cat.

9. Isobel 271-7625.
    she has the peace
    i want.

10. tea brewing
    dark as beer
    sharp as sticks.

11. i like to sample spices
    with a touch of one finger
    turning my mouth molten.

12. writes her
    phone number
    on his hand.

13. just made fun
    of him.
    for fun.

14. we sat on a bench.
    she offered me some chocolate.
    still warm from her hand.

15. i like that they make
    looking crazy look
    so good.

16. it's so shiny.
    i want it so much.
    i love it.

17. all my things
    begin to look
    like each other.

18. people get
    wound up like
    suckerpunches.

19. i ordered something.
    i feel like a
    big person now.

20. he functions
    as a kind of
    dare.

21.   a watch
       slit-slim
       on her wrist.

22.   down the street
       on his bike
       butt in the air.

23.   after my jogging.
       ready to take a shower.
       sweat underneath my boobs.

24.   swank fucks
       devouring sushi
       on friday night.

25.   even as i came
       i was holding
       something back.

26.   i like to call
       you my girlfriend.
       it's cute.

27.   kids crawling over fences
       peering into windows
       spying on boring people.

28.   i can't let go of
       it. it's too afraid
       to be free.

29.   the label's itchy.
       wants to let her body breathe.
       takes her panties off.

30.   holding back like
       someone who can't crash
       his car convincingly.

31.   we broke up.
       and why? because
       no reason.

32.   feeling so open
        in this short dress.
        want to take it off.

33.   that cat wants
        to kill things
        for me.

)) The Curl

34.   in bare feet
        she moves shoes
        in the window.

35.   he walks by her
        house. he will not
        look at it.

36.   morning rush.
        lets her hair dry
        on the way to work.

37.   in that window
        slit sheep on
        sharp hooks.

38.   beer helps me through this.
        big dull bridge over it.
        big hazy help.

39.   i smell odd things and
        sometimes odd things
        smell me.

40.   give me something
        to dance to underneath
        these sweet canopies.

41.   glossy magazine
        shimmies in light.
        cool appraisal.

42.   he puts his lips up
against the window and
blows wide as a moon.

43.   we wanted to kiss
in that dim light
in that lousy bar.

44.   active for an old guy.
checks out his
daughter's friends.

45.   do i need one?
but it's so good,
you should.

46.   how torrid.
in sock feet
she dances.

47.   sunny 11 a.m.
eyes closed, cat on
its back on the bed.

48.   your stay-up stockings
hug your thighs like rubber bands
around lobster claws.

49.   my good luck to have
a sociopath best friend.
you will be sorry.

50.   i need to piss.
but i just sit here
feeling it pulse.

51.   they screamed, threw panties.
danced down the aisles to the stage.
said everything.

52.   we lay on each
other like well-fed
polar bears.

53. twin sisters
     coordinating clothes
     unconsciously.

54. his young legs.
     like a girl's.
     confuses me.

55. she loves that
     dog who acts as
     if it owns her.

56. this frog pond poetry
     nothing like television.
     doesn't suck my cock.

57. she is taking a pee
     then coming here to
     where i am lying.

58. gold-digging and
     dumpster-diving among
     the filthy rich.

59. i'm not ready for
     this girl who could
     make me happy.

60. her pussy sits
     insane on my
     mouth.

61. meeting you
     a total fluke
     and fate.

62. someone wrote this
     thing i'm watching here
     with you now.

63. tottering in heels.
     down to the back of the bus.
     every man inhales.

64.   i stole this thing.
i could return it
with pain.

65.   i'm ready
to take revenge
on myself.

66.   his belt
so complex.
invites undoing.

67.   couldn't handle love.
i'm one of those
sorry bastards.

))) The Crash

68.   i only want to
start when i'm
already good at it.

69.   i'll be your dirty
old man if you'll
be my dirty old woman.

70.   beer on the porch
after work.
calm as grass.

71.   bringing in the clothes
my clothesline squeaking
gently jumping.

72.   i want the
cat downstairs
to visit me.

73.   a big man balding.
combs over the atlantic.
his hair tries so hard.

74.   we've eaten each other
       for so long we can't
       eat anyone else.

75.   the little pebbles
       stuck to my feet
       visit and fall off.

76.   my mundane
       uninteresting act of
       taking off my socks.

77.   them men in shirts
       and suits with cigars
       on the porch.

78.   fresh bagels
       warm as a cat
       on my lap.

79.   i want to go there.
       wherever there is
       in that picture.

80.   little kids running.
       doing weird movements
       distracting as teevee.

81.   skinny former dancer
       used to taking
       up space.

82.   see i can do this.
       say those things right back to you.
       i'm not afraid now.

83.   now stand back and
       let me see how pretty
       you all are.

84.   hot blonde.
       two things
       i'm not.

85. more living than
    dying today. more dawns
    than disasters.

86. your words are
    so big they don't
    fit past my teeth.

87. empty seat on
    the bus. weird
    stuff on it.

88. the kate moss of cats
    nudges me awake.
    wants love at 4 a.m.

89. all this ends the
    same way. me in a bowl
    on the sea.

90. a neighbourhood
    of open doors
    and ice cream.

91. nice carpet.
    i'd like it for myself
    in my house.

92. today made me
    forget what
    yesterday did.

93. even her.
    she's got her
    sexy bits.

94. that talent
    a neat toy
    i got long ago.

95. thanks to teevee i've
    seen a lot of different
    animals fuck.

96.   little kitten.
        a world of next
        corners.

97.   no heels today.
        non-honkable.

98.   she knows me
        well enough to be
        lazy with me.

99.   dog barks
        long after
        it needs to.

100.   each still-
        beating piece
        i have to eat.

ACKNOWLEDGEMENTS

You've seen some of these poems before. But very likely they were slightly different. Some have mutated since their initial publications in places such as *Quarry, Queen Street Quarterly, dig, UltraViolet, Kiss Machine, Word, Tupperware Sandpiper, Plastic Benjamin, Sum Magazine, The New Irregular, The Serialist Manifesto, The I.V. Lounge Reader,* and *Endnotes.*

I want to thank Mike O'Connor, Richard Almonte and Jan Barbieri at *Insomniac Press* for all their encouragement, patience, trust and unflagging support. One sip of Insomnia has me awake and hooked for life.

I want to thank Lynn Crosbie for helping to gather the ingredients necessary to make this loaf, and then agreeing to oversee its baking. You've been a great editor and a generous friend. Thank you for your words of encouragement and care. Thanks for the exercise in guts, for swimming freely where others drown.

Thanks to the numerous others who have supported me, helped me, and in whatever other form, loved me. I owe you everything. You're too numerous to list, so I intend to thank you in person.

I want to thank the angels.

I want to thank my family. My parents Boen-Min and Judy Tjia, and my brother Sean, who have supported me and seen me through virtually everything. Thank you all for having a keen awareness of how insane the world is, yet remaining remarkably calm in the midst of it. Thanks for letting me grow up in that. I now read the paper everyday with perfect equanimity.

I want to thank rYAN kAMSTRA & Margaux Wullumsum, the other two members of the *Groundfloor Artist's Collective,* and my pals for life. Thanks to sCRATCH for letting me steal relentlessly from him over the years. I hope I've managed to return the favour, if not the items. You're the wealthiest man I know. Thanks to MX. for being belly, better than jesus, and for kindly letting me use her incredible painting for the cover. Without you two, I would have quietly gone missing in 1999.

I want to thank Isabelle Marceau for all her love, kindness and continuing encouragement. Thank you also for letting me write weird poems about our lovely life. And thank you for letting me love you. You've made everything special.